HABITAT SURVIVAL

FORESTS

Claire Llewellyn

Chicago, Illinois

www.capstonepub.com
Visit our website to find out more information about Heinemann-Raintree books.

To order:

☎ Phone 800-747-4992

💻 Visit www.capstonepub.com
to browse our catalog and order online.

© 2013 Raintree
an imprint of Capstone Global Library, LLC
Chicago, Illinois

Edited by Nancy Dickmann, Kristen Kowalkowski, and Claire Throp
Designed by Philippa Jenkins
Original illustrations © Capstone Global Library Ltd 2013
Illustrations by Oxford Designers and Illustrators, and Jeff Edwards
Picture research by Tracy Cummins
Originated by Capstone Global Library Ltd
Printed and bound in China by CTPS

16 15 14 13
10 9 8 7 6 5 4 3 2

Library of Congress Cataloging-in-Publication Data
Llewellyn, Claire.
  Forests / Claire Llewellyn.
    p. cm.—(Habitat survival)
  Includes bibliographical references and index.
  ISBN 978-1-4109-4595-2 (hb)—ISBN 978-1-4109-4604-1 (pb) 1. Forest ecology—Juvenile literature. 2. Forests and forestry—Juvenile literature. 3. Forest animals—Juvenile literature. 4. Habitat (Ecology)—Juvenile literature. I. Title.
  QH541.5.F6L625 2013
  577.3—dc23   2012000233

Acknowledgments
We would like to thank the following for permission to reproduce photographs: Agefotostock p. 16 (© ARCO/D. Usher); FLPA pp. 8 (ImageBroker/Imagebroker), 12 (Donald M. Jones/Minden Pictures), 13 (Mark Sisson), 20 (Chien Lee/Minden Pictures), 21 (Suzi Eszterhas/Minden Pictures), 22 (Cyril Ruoso/Minden Pictures), 24 (Konrad Wothe/Minden Pictures), 27 (Paul Sawer), 29 (Murray Cooper/Minden Pictures); iStockphoto p. 15 (© Aleksander Bolbot); Nature Picture Library p. 28 (Eric Baccega); Shutterstock pp. 4 (© Rob Christiaans), 5 (© Poznyakov), 7 (© Andrew Roland), 10 (© Fokin Oleg), 11 (© sunnyfrog), 17 (© Irishman), 19 (© Dr. Morley Read), 25 (© Mary Terriberry), 26 (© Lisette van der Hoorn).

Cover photograph of a toucan reproduced with permission of Shutterstock/Vitaly Romanovich.

Contents

Some words are shown in bold, **like this**. You can find out what they mean by looking in the glossary.

What Are Forests?

Forests are big areas of land where trees grow close together, along with other kinds of plants. There are different kinds of forest around the world. This is because different **climates** suit different types of trees.

Forest life

Forests are important **habitats**. They provide animals with shelter and food. In fact, the more food a forest provides, the more kinds of animals will live in it. Many different animals live in the world's forests, from reindeer and wolves in the far north to tigers and snakes in the **tropics**.

Red deer live on the edges of **coniferous** forests. They feed on grasses, bushes, and young trees.

Parrots are just one of the many birds and animals that live in tropical rain forests.

This book looks at how plants and animals have **adapted** to life in the forest and how they depend on one another to survive. It examines how humans affect forests and how our actions can threaten forest life or help it to survive.

All sorts of life

Most forests contain a huge variety of plant and animal life. For example, scientists found 10,500 different kinds of animals and plants in a single forest in Switzerland.

Forests Around the World

In the far north, where it is bitterly cold, forests are made up of **evergreen** trees, such as firs and pines. Further south, where it is milder and wetter, forests contain more types of plants, and the trees lose their leaves in winter. In the **tropics**, there are steamy forests with tall trees and plants of every kind.

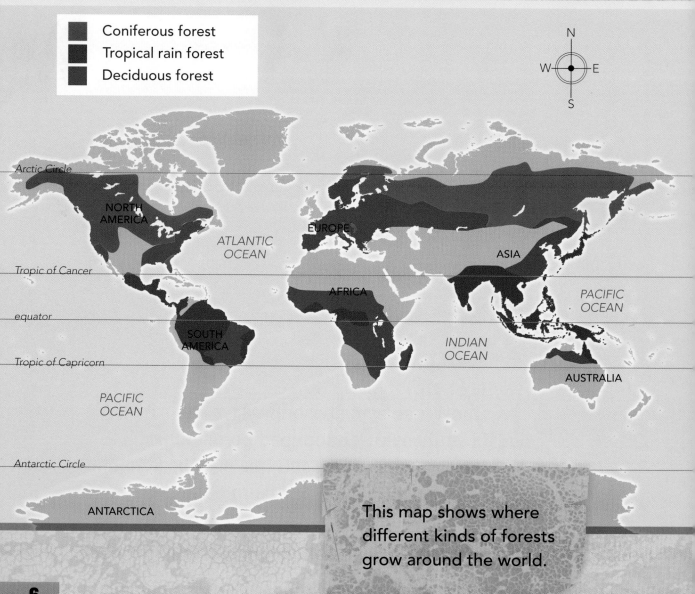

Coniferous forest
Tropical rain forest
Deciduous forest

N
W — E
S

Arctic Circle

NORTH
AMERICA

ATLANTIC
OCEAN

EUROPE

ASIA

Tropic of Cancer

AFRICA

PACIFIC
OCEAN

equator

SOUTH
AMERICA

INDIAN
OCEAN

Tropic of Capricorn

AUSTRALIA

PACIFIC
OCEAN

Antarctic Circle

ANTARCTICA

This map shows where different kinds of forests grow around the world.

A temperate forest changes in autumn. The leaves on the trees slowly change color and begin to fall to the ground.

Forest layers

Forests have different layers, similar to the floors in a building. On the ground, there are flowers and ferns. Next, there is the **understory**. It contains shrubs, small trees, **lichen**, and moss. At the top, the branches of the tallest trees make a green **canopy** over the forest. The different layers are home to different animals—from squirrels and monkeys high in the branches to beetles and worms on the ground.

Temperate rain forests

A different kind of rain forest grows in some cool, wet places, such as the north Pacific coast of the United States. These forests contain lush ferns and towering evergreen trees, which are covered with lichen and moss. They are called **temperate** rain forests.

The Forest Jigsaw

Everything in a forest depends on everything else. It is similar to a jigsaw puzzle made with four important pieces:

1. Plants: Plants use sunlight, air, and water to make food. They make leaves, bark, flowers, fruits, and seeds.

2. Plant eaters: Caterpillars, squirrels, deer, and many other animals eat the forest plants. They eat leaves, bark, flowers, berries, and nuts, as well as **lichen** and moss.

3. Meat eaters: Spiders, owls, and many other animals eat the plant eaters. They hunt smaller meat-eating animals, too.

4. Decomposers: When they die, animals and plants rot away with the help of **decomposers**, such as fungi, earthworms, and slugs. They turn dead things into **nutrients** for plants.

Owls are meat eaters. They feed on small **mammals**, such as mice and voles.

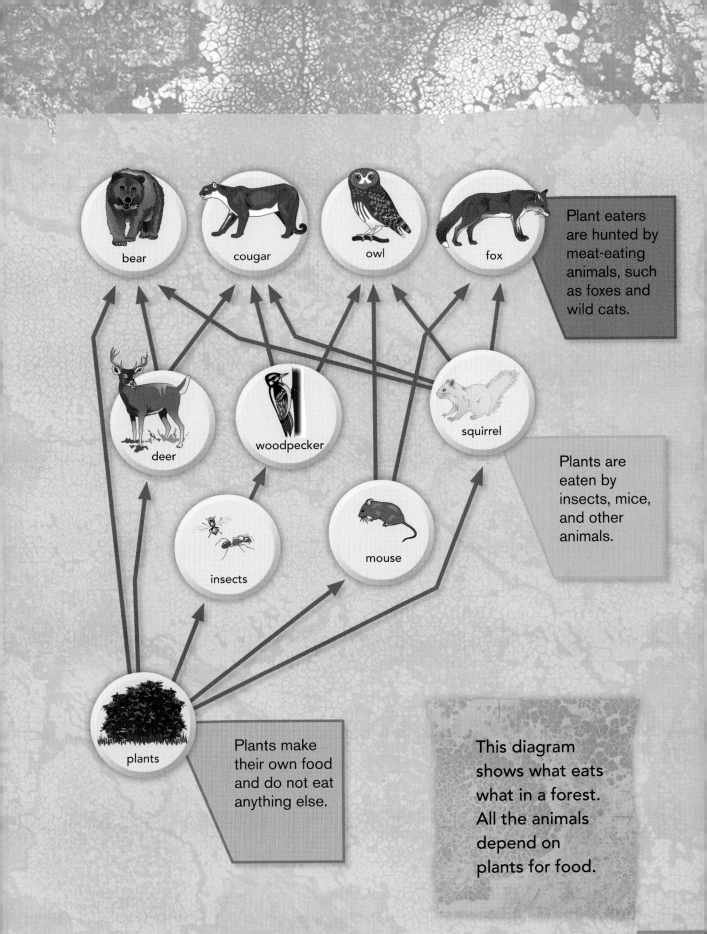

bear

cougar

owl

fox

Plant eaters are hunted by meat-eating animals, such as foxes and wild cats.

deer

woodpecker

squirrel

insects

mouse

Plants are eaten by insects, mice, and other animals.

plants

Plants make their own food and do not eat anything else.

This diagram shows what eats what in a forest. All the animals depend on plants for food.

Coniferous Forests

In the far north, a huge **evergreen** forest grows. The trees
are all **conifers**, such as fir and pine, and the forests are
called **coniferous** forests. These trees do not grow flowers.
Instead, they produce woody cones, which contain seeds.

Adapting to the cold

The conifers in northern forests have **adapted** to survive the
bitter cold. They have sloping branches to shed the snow and
needle-shaped leaves with a tough, waxy skin. These help the
trees to lock in water, which is scarce in winter.

Northern forests contain
only a few kinds of tree, but
they grow in vast numbers.

Conifers are different from other kinds of trees. They have needle-like leaves and woody cones.

On the ground

In northern forests, the ground is frozen for many months of the year. The surface of the soil **thaws** in summer, making the ground wet and spongy. It is covered with a thick mat of old pine needles. **Lichens** grow on the ground and on the branches of the trees.

Southern forests?

Conifers do grow south of the **equator**, but there are no huge coniferous forests. This is because the land there is too warm.

Animals in Coniferous Forests

Coniferous forests are not easy places for animals to live. There is very little food to eat, and the winters are long and cold.

Pine needles are not good to eat, so plant eaters, such as squirrels and birds, feed on the seeds inside the cones. Reindeer feed on **lichen** and moss. A reindeer's hooves are shaped like shovels to dig for lichen under the snow.

Crossbills have a crossed beak that works like a lever to open cones.

Meat eaters

Coniferous forests are home to pine martens. These fast animals chase birds and squirrels through the trees. They grip the bark with their strong claws, and their long tail helps them to balance as they leap from branch to branch. On the ground there are other hunters, such as wolves and bears.

Pine martens have good sight and hearing, and are well **adapted** to life in the trees.

Hiding food

Some birds hide seeds to last them through the winter. A nutcracker hides about 30,000 seeds a year in up to 5,000 different places! It remembers where most of them are, and the ones it forgets may grow into trees.

Deciduous Forests

South of the **coniferous** forests, there is a milder **climate** with plenty of rain. Forests have a greater mix of trees, such as oak, maple, ash, and beech. These trees grow broad, flat leaves, which fall to the ground in winter. They are called **deciduous** trees.

Leaves and roots

Deciduous trees grow new leaves in the spring. The trees have a spreading shape, which allows their leaves to reach the light. This provides them with **energy** to grow. Far below, in the ground, long roots suck up water and **nutrients** from the soil.

Energy from the Sun

A plant's leaves use sunlight, air, and water to make food.

Leaves take in **carbon dioxide** from the air

Roots take up water and nutrients

The damp forest floor is home to mosses and fungi.

The forest floor

In autumn, the days grow dark and there is not enough energy for the trees to grow. The leaves change color and fall to the ground. As they rot, they provide nutrients for trees, ferns, and shrubs.

Rings in the trunk

A deciduous tree makes new wood every year during the spring and summer. This shows up inside the trunk as rings, which can be seen when the tree is cut down. In good growing years, the rings are thick. In poor years, they are thin.

Animals in Deciduous Forests

The trees in a **deciduous** forest provide animals with plenty of leaves, fruits, and seeds to eat. Many more animals live here than in a **coniferous** forest.

Insects and birds

Deciduous trees are full of insects, such as beetles and wasps. Their young, which are called larvae, are food for birds. Woodpeckers use their long bills to drill into the trunks of trees and spear larvae feeding inside.

By eating harmful pests, such as larvae, woodpeckers keep trees healthy.

Brown bears eat well in summer and autumn. They hibernate through the winter, when there is not much food.

Forest mammals

Many **mammals** live in the forest, from squirrels and raccoons to weasels and deer. Bears spend most of their time on the ground but can climb trees to rest or feed in them. They eat almost every food the forest has to offer—nuts, honey, ants, eggs and chicks, and even young deer.

Is that a caterpillar?

Caterpillars are easy **prey** for birds, so they try to defend themselves. Some look like buds or twigs. Others blend in so well with their surroundings that they are hard to see.

17

Tropical Rain Forests

Tropical rain forests grow near the **equator**, in places that are warm all year round. Most days provide sunshine and rain. This kind of **climate** is perfect for plants.

In the Sun

Most rain forest trees are **evergreens** with broad leaves and tall, straight trunks. Their branches make a sunlit **canopy**, which produces leaves, flowers, and fruits. Other plants, such as orchids, perch high on the trees to reach the light. Their roots do not grow in the soil, but take in water from the steamy air.

The different layers of the rain forest are home to different kinds of plants—from fungi on the forest floor to orchids high in the trees.

orchid

liana

Canopy

Understory

In the shade

Below the canopy, in the **understory**, there is shade and dappled light. Small palm trees and banana plants grow here. Lower still, on the damp forest floor, fungi recycle old leaves and logs into **nutrients** for plants.

Below the canopy, there are ferns and woody vines, called lianas, which wind up toward the light.

All sorts of trees

In an area of rain forest the size of a football field, you might find 180 different kinds of tree. In a **deciduous** forest, you might find 10. In a **coniferous** forest, you would be lucky to find three.

Rain Forest Animals

Rain forests are home to many different animals. They have **adapted** to life at the different levels of the forest.

Monkeys run and leap through the trees. Many can use their tail as an extra arm or leg, by wrapping it around branches. Birds, bats, and butterflies fly from tree to tree. The flying lizard can glide, too. It stretches two flaps of skin, which work like wings.

Hiding away

Animals need to stay hidden as they hunt for **prey**. Their skin or fur helps them to do this. Bold markings help the gaboon viper to hide in the leaves on the forest floor. Big cats have coats with spots or stripes. This helps them to blend in with the forest's dappled light.

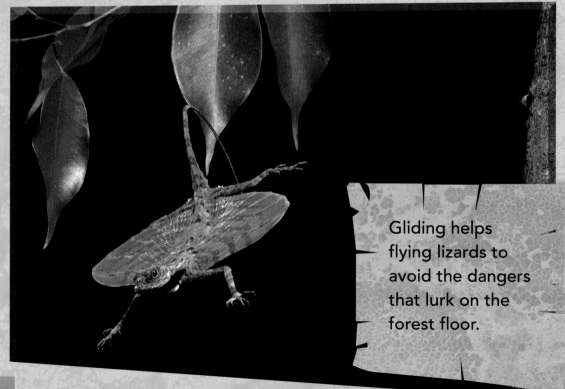

Gliding helps flying lizards to avoid the dangers that lurk on the forest floor.

The markings on a jaguar's coat blend in with the background, and make the cat harder to see.

On the ground

The forest floor is alive with creepy-crawlies. Armies of ants search for food. Large spiders, such as tarantulas, hunt for insects, frogs, and chicks. Deer and wild pigs search for leaves and roots.

Full of life

Tropical rain forests cover a very small area of Earth's surface. Yet scientists believe that they contain more than half of all the world's animals and plants.

Forest Tribes

People have lived in rain forests for thousands of years, and they still do today. Some forest tribes move from place to place. Others live in villages. They depend on the forest for many things.

The Baka tribe live in Cameroon, West Africa. They dry and weave the stalks and leaves of plants to make special clothing.

A world apart

About 200,000 people live in the rain forest in South America. Some live in such remote places that they have never had contact with the outside world.

Using plants

Forest people use hundreds of different plants. They use them to make their houses, clothes, and tools. They also collect them for medicines, fuel, and food. They gather pineapples, mangoes, nuts, and honey. They grow maize (corn) and other crops on small plots of land.

Catching animals

Forest people catch animals for food. They catch fish, gather insects, and hunt antelope, monkeys, and pigs. It takes great skill to stalk animals and shoot them with a bow and arrow, a spear, or a **poisoned** dart. Forest people make their own poisons from poisonous animals or plants.

Damaging the Forests

Humans are cutting down the world's forests. We use the wood to burn as fuel, to make buildings and furniture, and to make paper. We also clear forests to use the land for new houses and roads. All kinds of forests are disappearing, but tropical rain forests are in the greatest danger. Huge areas are cleared every year to make way for factories, mines, and farms. You now find cattle grazing on land where there was once thick forest.

When people cut down and burn tropical forests, animal and plant **habitats** are destroyed.

Acid rain threatens all kinds of forests. This problem is growing worse as there is more industry and more air pollution around the world.

Acid rain

Another way we damage forests is by air **pollution**. Factories and power stations give off dirty fumes. They mix with tiny drops of water in the air and form acid rain. On wet or foggy days, the acid rain lands on trees. It kills their leaves and weakens them, so they are less able to fight disease.

Disappearing forests

The world's forests are shrinking fast. In the last 300 years, the area of land that is covered by forests has been cut in half.

Forests Are Important

Forests are important for Earth's **climate**. Our planet is getting hotter as a result of **global warming**. This is caused by air **pollution**, which causes a buildup of **carbon dioxide** in the air. Forests can help with this problem. As trees make food for themselves, they remove carbon dioxide from the air. This helps slow down global warming.

These huge logs will be turned into timber.

Tigers in danger

Forests are important for the survival of animals. Amur tigers live in Russia's **coniferous** forests. People have built roads in the forests so they can cut down trees. However, the roads also help others to enter the forest and hunt these rare tigers for their skins.

Good for the environment

Trees are important for the **environment**. Their roots take in rainwater and hold the soil together. When forests are cut down, heavy rain runs away and often causes floods. It also washes the soil away.

Saving the Forests

Many people are working to protect forests. Some forests are turned into national parks. Scientists study animals there so they can understand their needs. For example, they put radio collars on **endangered** animals. This helps them to track the animals and protect them from hunters.

These forest rangers are fitting a radio collar to a black bear.

Planting trees

In the 1970s, Wangari Maathai from Kenya started an organization called the Green Belt Movement. It has helped people in Africa to plant over 40 million trees.

Protecting habitats

People will always need wood. If forests are cared for properly, we
can use them responsibly for our own needs as well as protect
plant and animal life. In some forests, people plant new trees to
replace the trees that have been cut down. These are called
sustainable forests.

Tourists pay money to see forest animals. If tourist numbers are
controlled, they do not harm these **habitats**, and their money can
be used to care for the forests. Forests are too important to lose,
and we must do all we can to protect them.

Glossary

adapt change in order to survive in a particular place

canopy top branches of trees in a forest that are very close together

carbon dioxide gas that is found in air

climate weather pattern in a particular part of the world

conifer evergreen tree that has needle-like leaves and grows its seeds inside cones

coniferous type of forest that contains only conifers

deciduous type of tree that loses its leaves in winter

decomposer animal that eats dead and rotting plants and animals

endangered threatened with dying out

energy power needed to grow, move, and live

environment surroundings in which an animal or plant lives

equator imaginary line around the widest part of Earth, where the weather is always warm

evergreen having leaves all year round

global warming increase in Earth's temperature, caused by chemicals in the air that trap the Sun's heat

habitat place where a plant or animal lives

lichen simple kind of plant that is half fungus and grows over walls and trees

mammal warm-blooded animal that usually has fur or hair and drinks milk from its mother when it is young

nutrient chemical in food that helps things to grow

poison substance that can cause illness or death

pollution spoiling the air, land, or water with harmful things such as plastic garbage

prey animal that is hunted and eaten by another animal

temperate area where temperatures are usually mild

thaw become soft as a result of warming up

tropics parts of the world that lie close to the equator

understory middle layer of a forest, between the canopy and the ground

Find Out More

Books

Hurtig, Jennifer. *Deciduous Forests* (Ecosystems). New York: Weigl Publishers, 2011.

Latham, Donna. *Coniferous Forests* (Endangered Biomes). White River Junction, Vt.: Nomad Press, 2011.

Newland, Sonya. *Woodland and Forest Animals* (Saving Wildlife). Mankato, Minn.: Smart Apple Media, 2012.

Pyers, Greg. *Biodiversity of Temperate Forests.* New York: Benchmark Books, 2011.

Internet Sites

Facthound offers a safe, fun way to find Internet sites related to this book. All of the sites on Facthound have been researched by our staff.

Here's all you do:

Visit *www.facthound.com*

Type in this code: 9781410945952

Index